Written by
Nick Hunter

Illustrated by
Jez Tuya

# CONTENTS

# RULED BY THE ROMANS

If you were born 1900 years ago, you would be living in Roman Britain. The Romans were fearsome fighters who built a huge **empire**. Rome started as a group of villages in Italy that grew into one big city. The Romans fought many wars to conquer new lands. People who tried to stop them ended up as slaves.

A Roman centurion was in charge of about 60–80 soldiers.

## GROWING UP GRIMLY

The Romans loved conquering new lands and celebrating victories, but slaves did most of the work. If you were living as a slave in Roman Britain, life was tough.

### DID YOU KNOW?

Romans used the same alphabet as us but their numbers looked very different. Here are the numbers from 1 to 12 as the Romans would have written them.

1 = I
2 = II
3 = III
4 = IV
5 = V
6 = VI
7 = VII
8 = VIII
9 = IX
10 = X
11 = XI
12 = XII

You can still see Roman ruins in many parts of Europe today. This is Hadrian's Wall, which is in the north of England.

**43 - 410**
ROMAN BRITAIN

**410 - 1066**
ANGLO-SAXON AND VIKING BRITAIN

**1066 - 1485**
NORMAN AND PLANTAGENET BRITAIN

**1485 - 1603**
TUDOR BRITAIN

**1603 - 1714**
STUART BRITAIN

**1714 - 1837**
GEORGIAN BRITAIN

**1837 - 1901**
VICTORIAN BRITAIN

**1901 - 1918**
EDWARDIAN BRITAIN AND WORLD WAR I

**1920 - 1945**
THE TWENTIES, THIRTIES AND WORLD WAR II

## RULING BRITAIN

Rainy Britain was very different from hot, sunny Rome but the terrible weather didn't stop the Romans from ruling Britain for 400 years.

# WAKING UP IN ROMAN BRITAIN

Winter mornings would have seemed even colder and darker in Roman Britain than they do nowadays. There were no electric lights for dark mornings, or comfy duvets to snuggle up in. Rich Romans had beds with thick mattresses fixed to a frame with leather straps. Most slaves could only dream about this luxury.

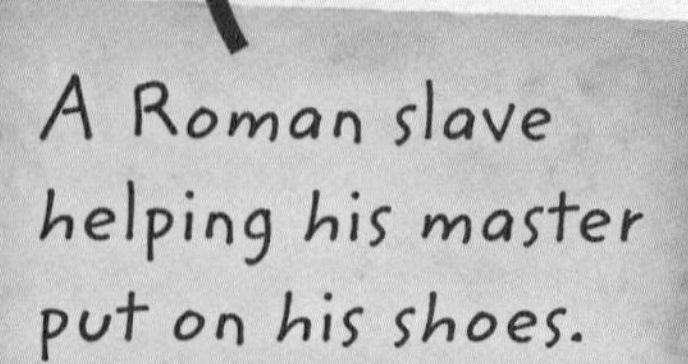

A Roman slave helping his master put on his shoes.

Imagine you are a slave in Roman Britain. You are eight years old and there are no lazy lie-ins for you!

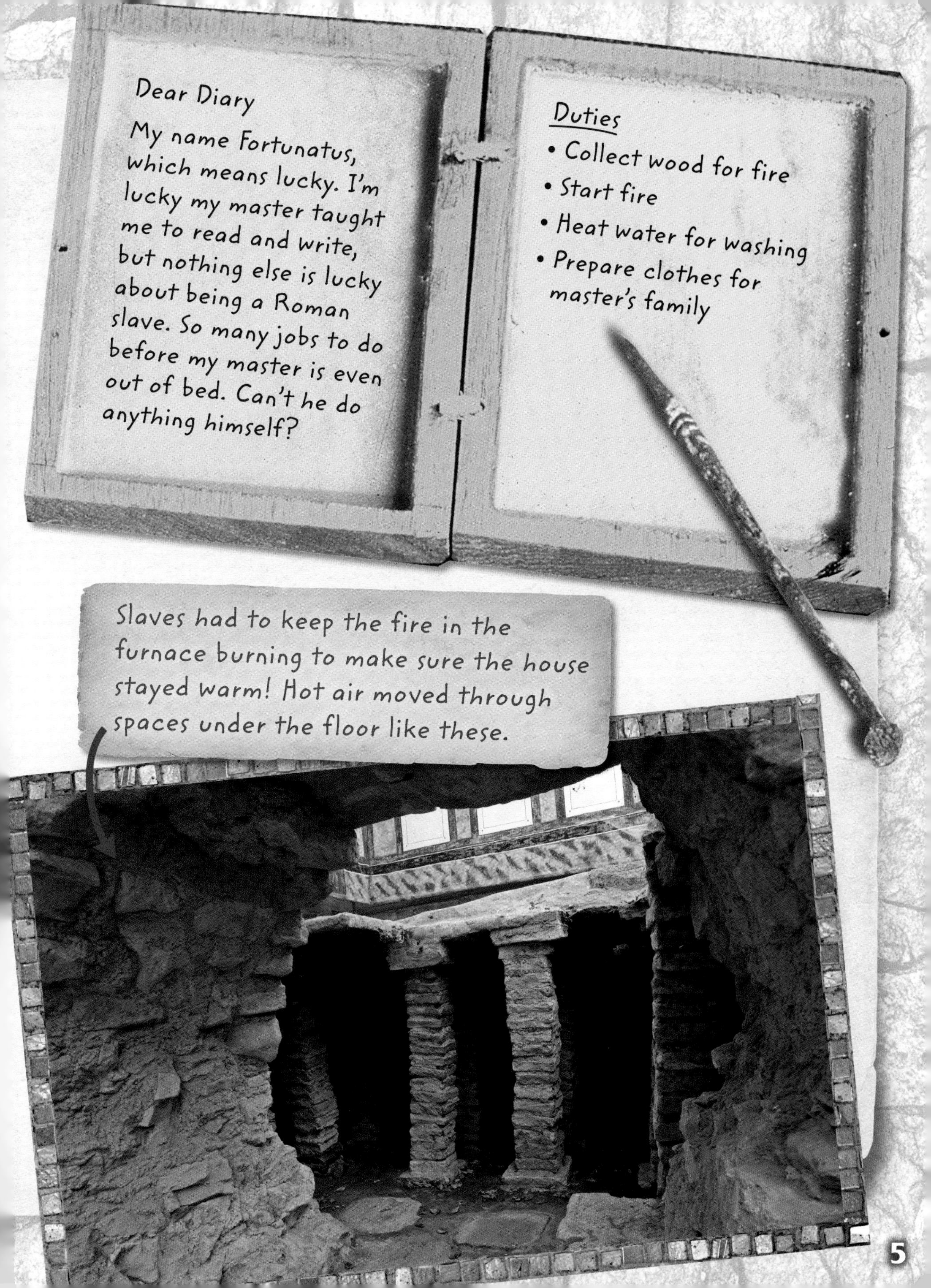

Dear Diary

My name Fortunatus, which means lucky. I'm lucky my master taught me to read and write, but nothing else is lucky about being a Roman slave. So many jobs to do before my master is even out of bed. Can't he do anything himself?

Duties

- Collect wood for fire
- Start fire
- Heat water for washing
- Prepare clothes for master's family

Slaves had to keep the fire in the furnace burning to make sure the house stayed warm! Hot air moved through spaces under the floor like these.

# TERRIBLE TUNICS AND SMELLY SANDALS

How long does it take you to get dressed? A Roman slave was very quick. When he put on his rough, itchy woollen tunic, he was ready for the day.

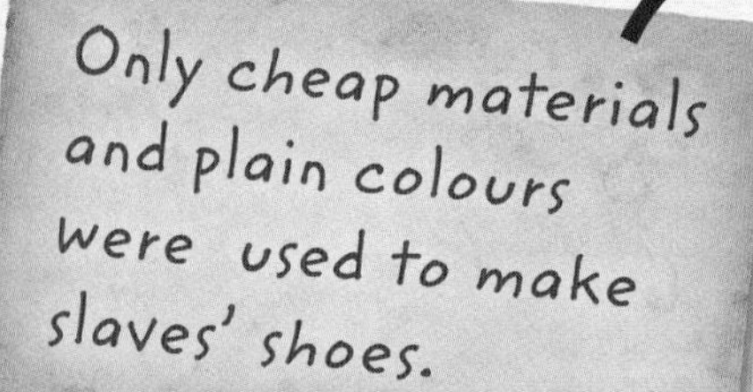

Only cheap materials and plain colours were used to make slaves' shoes.

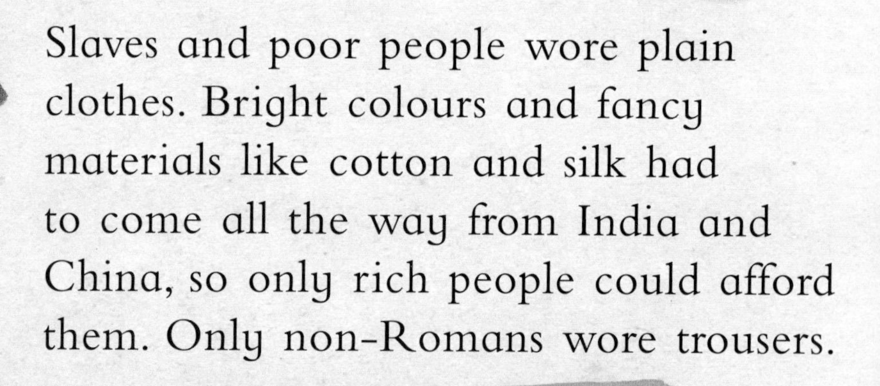

Slaves and poor people wore plain clothes. Bright colours and fancy materials like cotton and silk had to come all the way from India and China, so only rich people could afford them. Only non-Romans wore trousers.

The tunics worn by men, women and children were made of wool but did not give much protection from the cold wind in Britain.

# DRESSING LIKE YOUR DAD

Do you dress like your parents? Sounds pretty dull – but Roman children had no choice. On festival days, boys wore long, woollen **togas** just like their dads. Women and girls loved fancy hairstyles and jewellery.

Romans wore leather sandals with woollen socks. They really did dress like my dad!

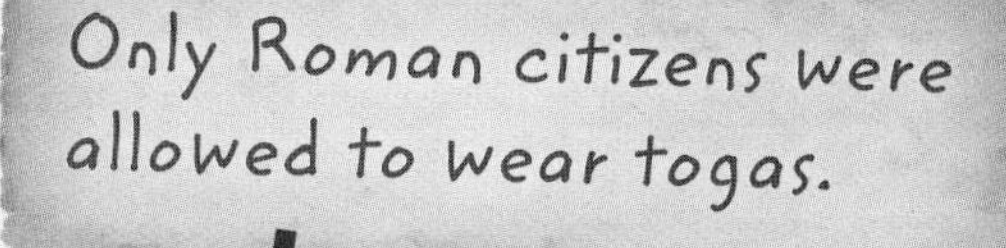


Dear Diary

Another feast day today – whole family had to wear best clothes. Togas had to be gleaming white and arranged just right. They are made from long sheets of woollen cloth and are almost impossible to keep clean.

# MEET THE FAMILY

What do you have for breakfast? There wasn't much to choose from at a Roman breakfast. There was no breakfast cereal, toast, or even sugar. Romans ate a simple breakfast of bread or fruit. People with a sweet tooth might add a bit of honey. One thing about Roman breakfast would be familiar – everyone was in a hurry.

Families in Roman Britain usually only had one or two children because so many died young.

If you were a slave, you would be lucky to have a quick breakfast of bread and water before starting work. Your next meal wouldn't be until the evening when all your work was done.

## A BUSY DAY

Fathers of richer families rushed off to work or business meetings. Boys who went to school had to be there at dawn. Girls learned how to manage a house from their mothers, including how to order the slaves around.

## DID YOU KNOW?

Roman fathers had total power over their children. They could even decide if newborn babies lived or died ...

## OUTNUMBERED

In the richest households, there would be more slaves than family members.

Skilled slaves knew how to create fancy hairstyles that Roman women and girls wanted.

## THINK ABOUT IT!

### Roman girls

Imagine being a girl in Roman Britain. Many girls were expected to marry and start having their own families by the age of 14. Boys did not get married until their twenties.

# DUSTING THE MOSAICS

Romans had to pay to go to school. Only rich families could afford it, and they did not usually spend money teaching slaves to read and write. Slave children could look forward to days of work, work and more work.

## TIME TO CLEAN

Do you help clean your home? Cleaning a large Roman house was a big job. Slaves had no vacuum cleaners or dishwashers. The Romans really knew how to make a mess, especially in the front rooms where the family entertained guests.

Our mistress is expecting guests for dinner. She has given strict instructions:

- Dust the mosaics.
- Scrub clean the eating couches.
- Wipe the best glass tableware.

She wants her guests to know how rich the family is. Some of the glass dishes cost more than I did!

Mosaics were made of hundreds of tiny tiles.

## THINK ABOUT IT!

### Toilet habits

Imagine having no toilet paper. Romans used a sponge on a stick to wipe their bottoms! Only the wealthiest homes had toilets. Slaves would have to make do with a hole in the ground.

# SCARY SCHOOLS

Everyone wants a day off school sometimes, but imagine if you never had the chance to go to school to learn to read and write and count. That's what happened to most slave children in Roman Britain.

For Romans, though, school started early and went on until early afternoon. Roman lessons might seem boring to us. There were no whiteboards, computers or even books. The children just had to sit and listen while their teacher spoke in the Roman language, Latin. Children would learn to read from a scroll made of animal skin. They wrote on a **wax tablet** with a stick called a stylus.

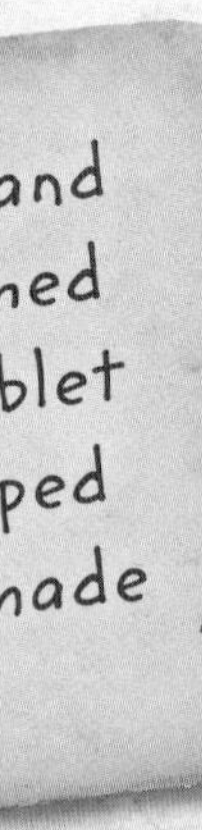

Latin words and sums scratched on a wax tablet could be wiped off if you made a mistake.

## DID YOU KNOW?

**Graffiti**

Romans who could write sometimes scrawled graffiti around their towns. They included love poems, advertisements for gory games, and horrible insults.

I'm glad I'm not a Roman school child. I would have been beaten with a cane for being late, or for getting my sums wrong.

A Roman school was usually just a small group of children. Teachers were often educated slaves.

# BLISSFUL BATH TIME

Romans liked nothing better than a soak in a hot bath. They then jumped straight into a freezing cold bath! In Roman Britain, bathing meant taking a bath with your friends. Don't worry – the bath was big enough for everyone! Women and children went to the public bath-house in the morning. Men went after work. It was a place to meet, chat and play, as well as to keep clean.

You can still see some Roman baths in Bath.

# A QUICK BATH?

There was no such thing as a quick bath in Roman Britain! Bathers moved through several different rooms.

Leave clothes in changing room

Move through several hot rooms getting sweatier each time

Cover the body in smelly oil

Scrape off oil and dirt with a strigil

Relax in a hot bath

Jump into a very cold bath

Hope that the slave guard has stopped your clothes being stolen!

a strigil

Most mornings I have to go to the baths with my mistress and her children. Bath-time takes ages – but at least I can leave the hard work of washing my mistress and the children to the slaves in the bath house!

## THINK ABOUT IT!

### Roman toothpaste

Imagine cleaning your teeth with a mixture of crushed eggshells, oyster shells and bones! Roman toothpaste was definitely not 'fresh and minty'.

# WATCH WHERE YOU'RE WALKING!

Housework and bathing are done. Now it's time to go shopping. There were no buses or cars in Roman Britain. Ordinary people and slaves walked. At least the Romans built good roads, although people had to dodge the muck left by horses and animals on their way to market.

The towns of Britain were small and shabby compared to beautiful cities elsewhere in the Roman empire. However, before the Romans arrived, there had been no towns at all in Britain. New public buildings, like the **forum**, would have impressed the Britons.

Stepping stones helped people keep their feet clean when they crossed the road.

THINK ABOUT IT!

## Travelling in style

Imagine being on a Roman street and seeing a person travelling in a large carriage being carried by people. This was called a litter and was the grandest and cleanest way to travel. Only very important people travelled this way.

# STOP AT THE SHOPS

What do you do when you are hungry? Do you just look in the fridge for something to eat? There were no fridges to keep food fresh in Roman Britain. Slaves had to buy food at the market every day.

The market bustled with people and produce from as far away as Africa and Spain. The goods were not packaged up but laid out in front of the traders.

Market traders set up their stalls in the forum or in a market hall.

## FUNNY MONEY

The market traders only accepted coins with the head of the current **emperor** on them. You needed to check your change in case the trader tried to give you coins showing a previous emperor.

These coins show the heads of different Roman emperors.

Shopping list

I'll never get the hang of these Roman numbers. Here's my shopping list:

I (1) large pot of fish sauce
II (2) bags of flour
V (5) bunches of grapes
X (10) oranges
XII (12) eggs

THINK ABOUT IT!

### Slave market

Imagine finding people on sale in your local market. The Romans thought nothing of buying and selling slaves, including children. How the slaves were treated depended on who bought them.

# NO JOB FOR A CHILD

House slaves had an easy life compared to some. Children working on farms in the country had to do back-breaking work in the fields. Some jobs were even worse than that.

The smaller the children, the more easily they could fit in the dark tunnels.

## DOWN THE MINES

The worst place to be a young slave was in the silver and lead mines. Children as young as four worked underground with tiny axes and buckets. They were often killed by falling rocks.

Silver was mined to make beautiful jewellery for the rich.

## ROMAN LAUNDRY

**Fuller** slaves helped to clean Roman clothes, a bit like modern dry cleaners. That doesn't sound too bad, does it? To do the cleaning they had to collect pots full of wee from street corners and public toilets. Then they trod on the clothes in a mixture of wee and water to clean them!

## SICK COLLECTOR

The worst job in the house for a slave was the sick collector. This lucky boy or girl had to clean up the sick and spit that the disgusting Romans left after a really big feast!

# GORY GAMES

There was one kind of school that no slave wanted to go to – gladiator school. There, gladiators learned to fight wild animals, and each other, in front of huge, cheering crowds.

## ROMAN GAMES

The games lasted all day but the Romans really loved the gladiator fights in the afternoon.

Games Programme

Morning: Hunters vs wild animals, including Scottish bears

Lunchtime: **Execution** of criminals

Afternoon: gladiator contests and thrilling fights to the death!

REFRESHMENTS AVAILABLE.
BRING YOUR OWN CUSHION.

Some gladiators became heroes like modern sport stars, but the next fight could always be their last!

# CHARIOTEERING DREAMS

Many slave boys dreamed of being charioteers. **Chariot** racing was the Formula 1 of its day, with up to 12 chariots battling for victory, cheered on by screaming fans. Charioteers could become rich and famous while they were still teenagers. They could also die young in horrific, high-speed crashes.

Roman chariots were fast and light, with only a thin, waist-height barrier between the charioteer and horses.

## THINK ABOUT IT!

### Crashing out

Imagine being a charioteer racing around a track. But what if you crashed? The only safety gear a charioteer carried was a small knife for cutting the reins so he wasn't dragged around behind his horses.

# PLAYTIME

After school, Roman children got a chance to play. The closest slaves got to playtime was tidying up after their master's children.

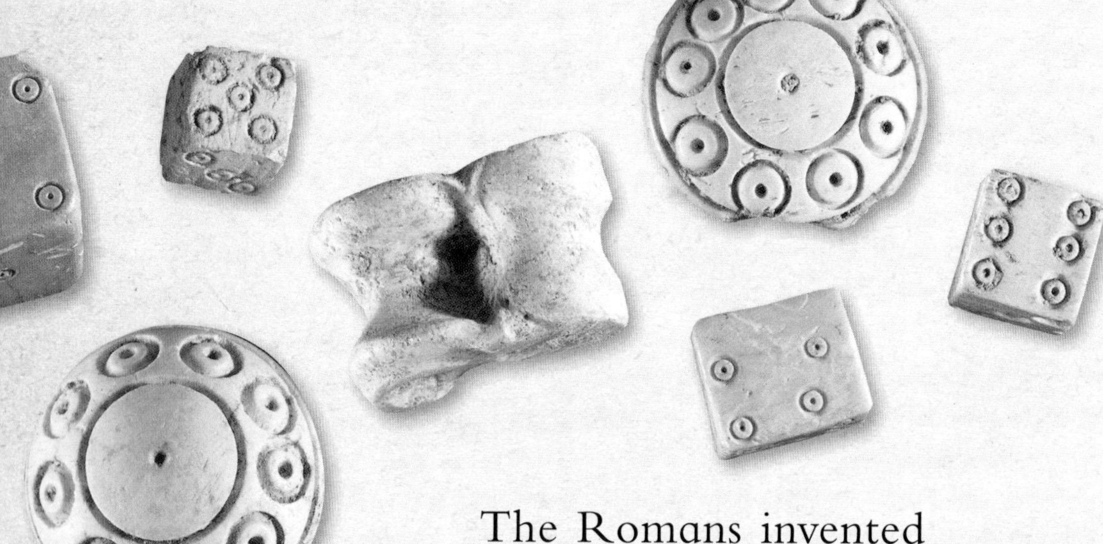

Roman dice, counters and knucklebones

The Romans invented scooters and yo-yos, but most of their toys were a bit more basic. How would you like it if you only had rag dolls and animals made from wood or pottery to play with? Some lucky children had toy chariots that were pulled around by mice.

## DID YOU KNOW?

**The Romans brought a rough ball game called harpastum to Britain. Eventually, this game changed to become modern football.**

These children are playing knucklebones.

Knucklebones

If we slaves get a chance to relax, we play a game of knucklebones. All you need are the bones from the feet of sheep (or some pebbles).

- Boil the sheep's feet until the flesh falls off the small knucklebones.
- Throw the bones (or pebbles) up into the air.
- See how many you can catch on the back of your hand.

# DO YOU WANT THAT DORMOUSE STUFFED?

What's your favourite food? How about peacock's brains, flamingo's tongue or sauce made with fish guts? Romans who could afford it liked to be adventurous with their meals.

Slaves started to prepare the family's evening meal in the afternoon. At a Roman dinner party, there were lots of little courses. Meals could last for hours.

Romans ate their dinner lying on couches around a table.

## TERRIBLE TABLE MANNERS

At the end of the meal, each diner would burp and break wind to show how much they'd enjoyed it!

## DID YOU KNOW?

**At one emperor's dinner party, so many rose petals dropped from the ceiling that some guests could not breathe and died.**

# SWEET DREAMS

Finally, when the lengthy dinner was over, Romans would settle down to watch TV. Just kidding! Once it was dark, everyone went to bed. Candles or lamps burning olive oil did not give much light. Anyway, they all had to be up again at dawn.

Lying in their tiny rooms at the back of the house, slave boys and girls would dream about one day winning their freedom. They could be given freedom by their master or they could buy themselves out of slavery if they earned money in business. Until then, all they could look forward to were festivals like **Saturnalia**.

Many Roman slaves didn't have their own room, but slept in the cellar, the kitchen or even the corridors!

Saturnalia celebrated the Roman god of farming, wealth and freedom.
Dear Diary,
Happy Saturnalia! For a whole week slaves are part of the family. We even get presents. I got a little statue of the god Saturn!
Saturnalia sounds a bit like Christmas. I would not be pleased if I got a statue as a present.

# SURVIVING A ROMAN CHILDHOOD

Growing up in Roman Britain was tough and could be dangerous. Here are some tips to stay alive and get ahead:

Don't be a slave: some slaves became rich, but more ended up working in mines.

Be a boy: boys had most of the fun in Roman Britain. But at least girls couldn't end up as gladiators.

Listen to your dad: Roman dads expected to be obeyed – best just to agree.

Watch what you eat: peacock's brain and rotting fish sauce may not taste as bad as they sound, but they do sound really disgusting.

Don't race chariots or become a gladiator.

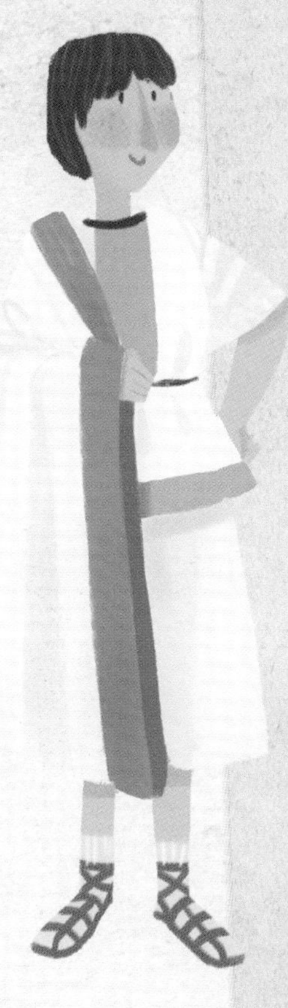

# HAPPY BIRTHDAY!

If they survived, Roman boys marked their 16th birthdays with a special ceremony. They were given a grown-up toga and became adults. Girls were often already married. Slaves, of course, just carried on being slaves.

When they became men, boys gave up their lucky bulla charm they wore in childhood.

# GLOSSARY

**chariot** two-wheeled racing cart pulled by horses

**emperor** king that rules over an empire

**empire** lands or colonies ruled from another country

**execution** killing someone as punishment for a crime

**forum** the town square where important people ran the government

**fuller** person who cleaned togas and other cloth

**Saturnalia** Roman festival held in December

**strigil** scraper used to scrape dirt off the skin

**wax tablet** writing surface covered with soft wax

# INDEX